RUBANK EDUCATIONAL LIBRARY No. 158

Rubank Advanced Method

CORNET OR TRUMPET

Vol. II

WM. GOWER
AND
H. VOXMAN

AN OUTLINED COURSE OF STUDY
DESIGNED TO FOLLOW UP ANY
OF THE VARIOUS ELEMENTARY
AND INTERMEDIATE METHODS

HAL•LEONARD® CORPORATION
7777 W. BLUEMOUND RD. P.O.BOX 13819 MILWAUKEE, WI 53213

NOTE

THE RUBANK ADVANCED METHOD for Cornet or Trumpet is published in two volumes, the course of study being divided in the following manner:

Vol. I
- Keys of C, F, G, B♭, and D Major.
- Keys of A, D, E, G, and B Minor.

Vol. II
- Keys of E♭, A, A♭, E, D♭, and B Major.
- Keys of C, F♯, F, and C♯ Minor.

PREFACE

THIS METHOD is designed to follow any of the various Elementary and Intermediate instruction series, or Elementary instruction series comprising two or more volumes, depending upon the previous development of the student. The authors have found it necessary in their teaching experience to draw from many sources in order to provide a progressive course of study. The present publication assembles in two volumes, the material essential to a well-rounded musical development.

THE OUTLINES, one of which is included in each of the respective volumes, tend to afford an objective picture of the student's progress. They will facilitate the ranking of members in a large ensemble or they may serve as a basis for awards of merit. In addition, a one-sided development along strictly technical or strictly melodic lines is avoided. The use of these outlines, however, is not imperative and they may be discarded at the discretion of the teacher.

Wm. Gower — H. Voxman

CHROMATIC FINGERING CHART
for Cornet and Trumpet

① The C♯ or D♭ below the staff is too sharp. Flatten this tone enough to make it in good tune.

② The D on the fourth line is usually too flat. In slow passages this may be improved by using the 1st and 3rd valves.

③ The E on the fourth space is sometimes too flat. Use the 1st and 2nd valves to correct this.

TABLE OF HARMONICS

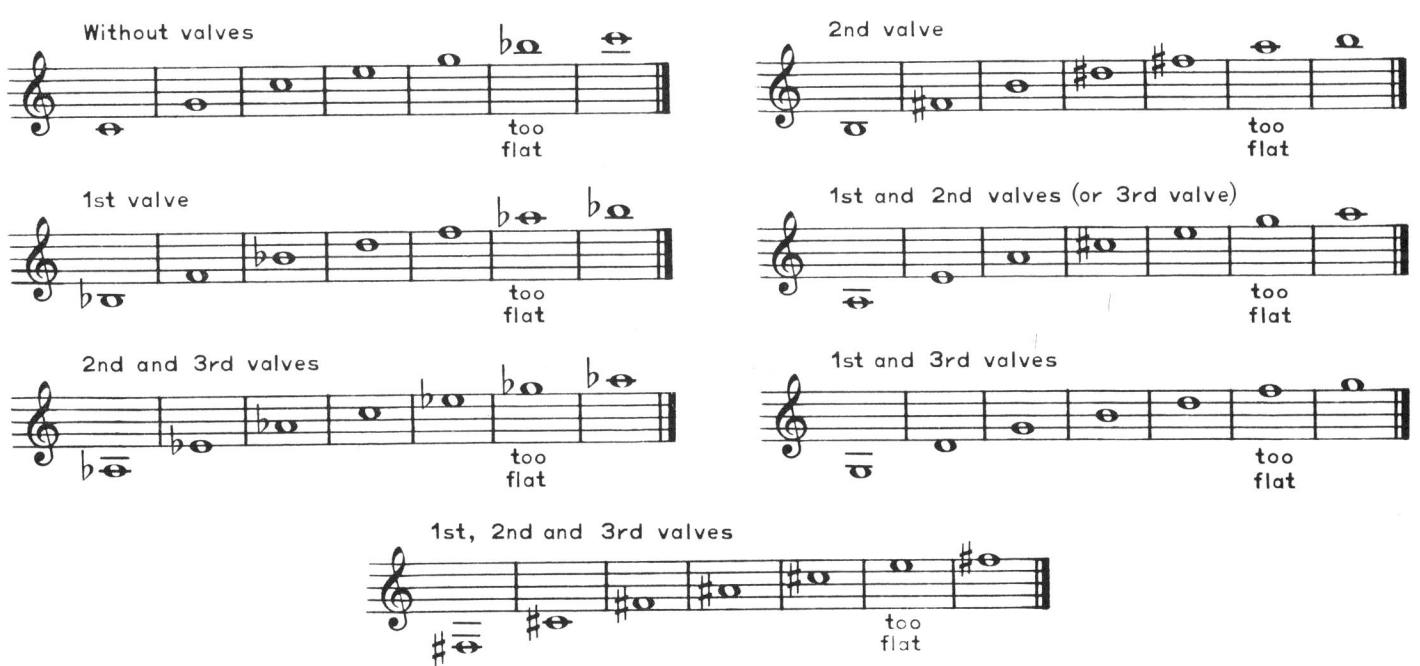

Fingerings for the tones above high C:

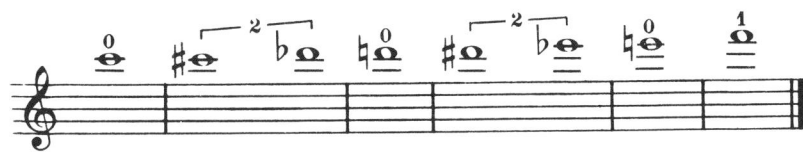

Copyright MCMLIV by Rubank, Inc., Chicago, Ill.
International Copyright Secured

PRACTICE AND GRADE REPORT

SECOND SEMESTER

Student's Name: _____ Date: _____

Week	Sun.	Mon.	Tue.	Wed.	Thu.	Fri.	Sat.	Total	Parent's Signature	Grade
1										
2										
3										
4										
5										
6										
7										
8										
9										
10										
11										
12										
13										
14										
15										
16										
17										
18										
19										
20										

Semester Grade: _____

Instructor's Signature: _____

FIRST SEMESTER

Student's Name: _____ Date: _____

Week	Sun.	Mon.	Tue.	Wed.	Thu.	Fri.	Sat.	Total	Parent's Signature	Grade
1										
2										
3										
4										
5										
6										
7										
8										
9										
10										
11										
12										
13										
14										
15										
16										
17										
18										
19										
20										

Semester Grade: _____

Instructor's Signature: _____

OUTLINE OF RUBANK ADVANCED METHOD FOR CORNET or TRUMPET, Vol. II
BY Wm. Gower and H. Voxman

UNIT	SCALES and ARPEGGIOS (Key)				MELODIC INTERPRE-TATION	ARTICU-LATION	FLEXIBILITY and TONGUING		ORNA-MENTS	SOLOS	UNIT COMPLETED
1	6	①	7	⑤	E♭	20 ①	44 ①	56 ①	60 ①	66 ①	73 ①	
2	6	②	7	⑥	E♭	21 ②	44 ②	56 ①	60 ①	66 ②	73 ①	
3	6	③	7	⑦	E♭	22 ③	45 ③	56 ①	60 ②	66 ②	73 ①	
4	7	④	⑧		E♭	22 ③	45 ③	56 ②	60 ③	66 ③	73 ①	
5	8	⑨			c	23 ④	46 ④	56 ②	60 ③	66 ③	73 ①	
6	8	⑩			c	24 ⑤	46 ⑤	56 ②	60 ④	67 ④	73 ①	
7	8	⑪	⑫	⑬	c	24 ⑤	46 ⑤	57 ③	60 ⑤	67 ④	74 ②	
8	8	⑭	10	⑱	A	25 ⑥	46 ⑥	57 ③	60 ⑤	67 ⑤	74 ②	
9	9	⑮	10	⑲	A	26 ⑦	47 ⑦	57 ④	61 ⑥	67 ⑥	74 ②	
10	9	⑯	10	⑳	A	27 ⑧	47 ⑧	57 ④	61 ⑥	67 ⑥	74 ②	
11	9	⑰	10	㉑	A	27 ⑧	47 ⑧	57 ⑤	61 ⑦	68 ⑦ ⑧	74 ②	
12	10	㉒	㉓		f♯	28 ⑨	47 ⑨	57 ⑤	61 ⑦	68 ⑨	74 ②	
13	11	㉔	㉕		f♯	28 ⑩	48 ⑩	57 ⑥	62 ⑧	68 ⑩	76 ③	
14	11	㉖	㉗	㉘	f♯	28 ⑩	48 ⑩	57 ⑥	62 ⑧	68 ⑩	76 ③	
15	12	㉙			A♭	29 ⑪	48 ⑪	57 ⑥	62 ⑨	69 ⑪ ⑫	76 ③	
16	12	㉚	13	㉝	A♭	30 ⑫	48 ⑫	57 ⑥	62 ⑨	69 ⑬	76 ③	
17	12	㉛	13	㉞	A♭	30 ⑬	49 ⑬	57 ⑦	62 ⑨	69 ⑭	76 ③	
18	12	㉜	13	㉟	A♭	30 ⑬	49 ⑬	57 ⑦	63 ⑩	69 ⑮	76 ③	
19	13	㊱	㊲		f	32 ⑭	50 ⑭	57 ⑦	63 ⑩	69 ⑯	77 ④	
20	13	㊳	14	㊵	f	32 ⑮	50 ⑮	58 ⑧	63 ⑪	69 ⑯	77 ④	
21	14	㊴	㊶	㊷	f	32 ⑮	50 ⑮	58 ⑧	63 ⑪	70 ⑰	77 ④	
22	14	㊸	15	㊻	E	33 ⑯	51 ⑯	58 ⑧	63 ⑫	70 ⑰	77 ④	
23	14	㊹			E	34 ⑰	51 ⑰	58 ⑧	63 ⑫	70 ⑱	77 ④	
24	15	㊺			E	34 ⑱	51 ⑰	58 ⑧	63 ⑬	70 ⑱	77 ④	
25	15	㊼	㊽		E	34 ⑱	52 ⑱	58 ⑨	64 ⑭	70 ⑲	78 ⑤	
26	15	㊾	㊿		c♯	36 ⑲	52 ⑲	58 ⑨	64 ⑭	71 ⑳	78 ⑤	
27	16	㊑	㊓		c♯	37 ⑳	53 ⑳	58 ⑨	64 ⑮	71 ⑳	78 ⑤	
28	16	㊒	㊔	㊕	c♯	37 ⑳	53 ⑳	58 ⑨	64 ⑮	71 ㉑	78 ⑤	
29	16	㊖			D♭	38 ㉑	53 ㉑	58 ⑨	64 ⑯	72 ㉒	78 ⑤	
30	17	㊗	18	㊠	D♭	38 ㉒	54 ㉒	58 ⑨	64 ⑯	72 ㉒	78 ⑤	
31	17	㊘	18	㊡	D♭	40 ㉓	54 ㉓	59 ⑩	65 ⑰	72 ㉓	80 ⑥	
32	17	㊙	18	㊢	D♭	40 ㉓	54 ㉓	59 ⑩	65 ⑰	72 ㉔	80 ⑥	
33	18	㊣	19	㊧	B	41 ㉔	55 ㉔	59 ⑩	65 ⑱	72 ㉕	80 ⑥	
34	18	㊤	19	㊨	B	41 ㉔	55 ㉔	59 ⑩	65 ⑱	72 ㉖	80 ⑥	
35	19	㊥	㊩		B	43 ㉕	55 ㉕	59 ⑩	65 ⑲	72 ㉗	80 ⑥	
36	19	㊦	㊪		B	43 ㉕	55 ㉕	59 ⑩	65 ⑲	72 ㉘	80 ⑥	

NUMERALS designate page number.
ENCIRCLED NUMERALS designate exercise number.
COMPLETED EXERCISES may be indicated by crossing out the rings, thus, .

Scales and Arpeggios
E♭ Major

4

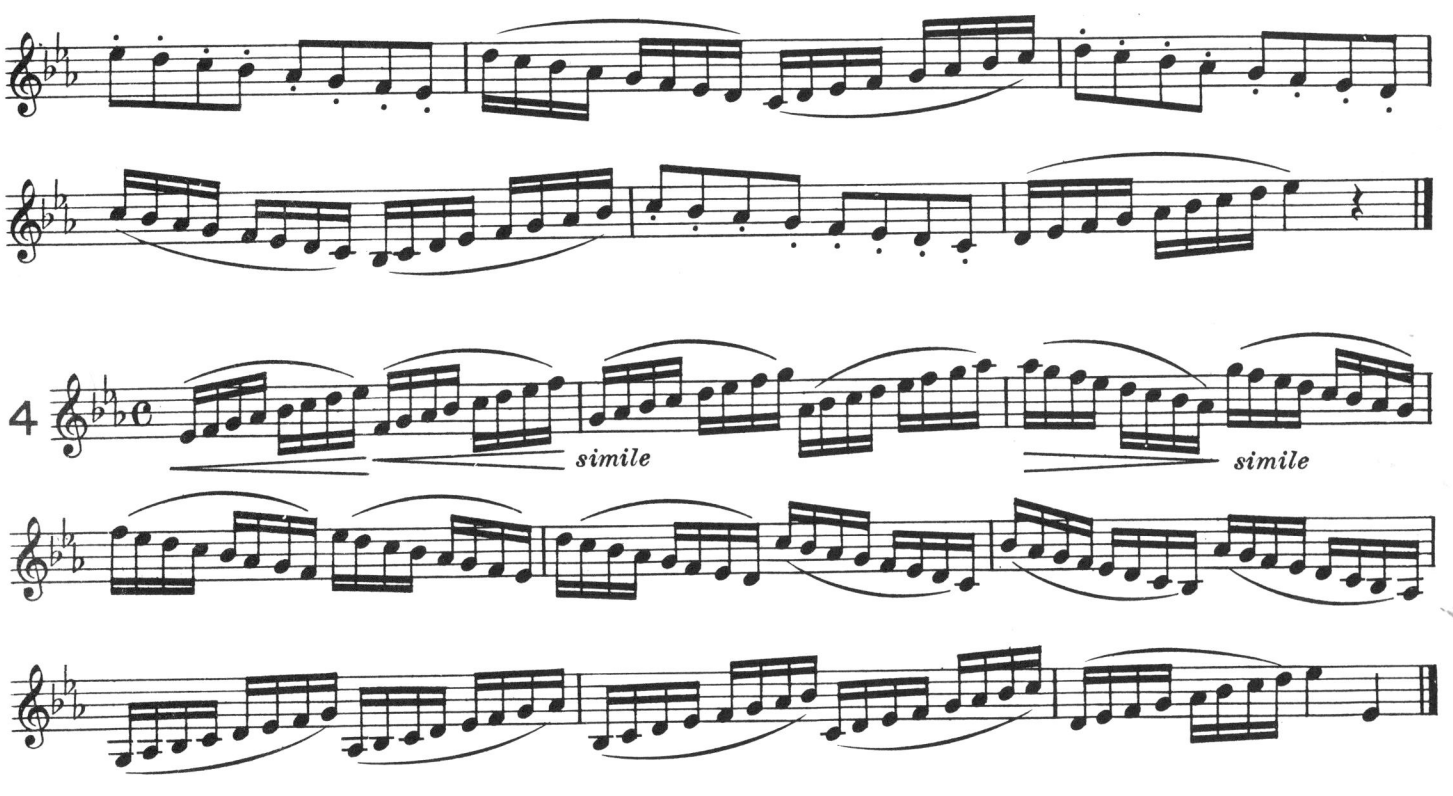

Various articulations may be used in the chromatic, the interval, and the arpeggio exercises.

Chromatic Scale

5 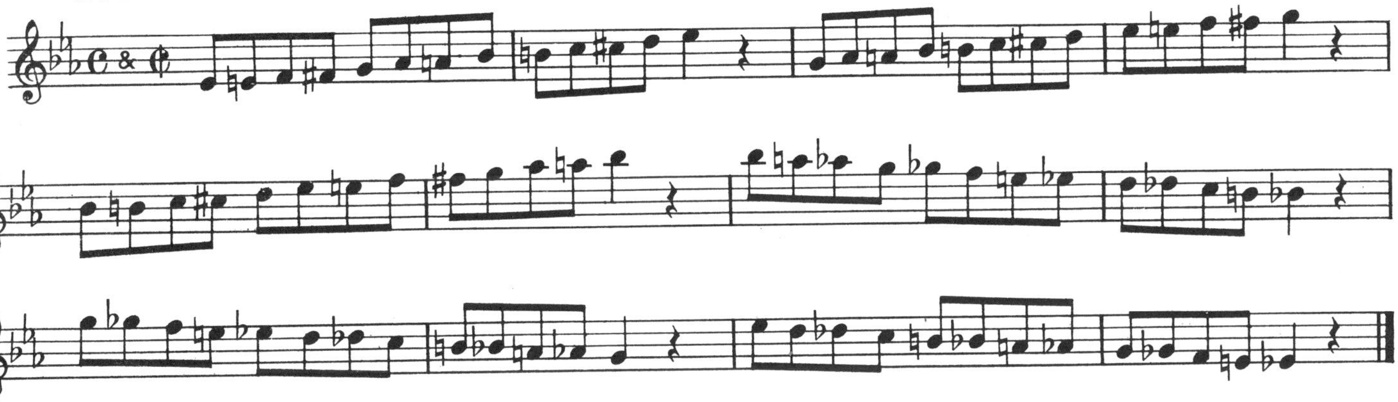

Exercise in Thirds

6 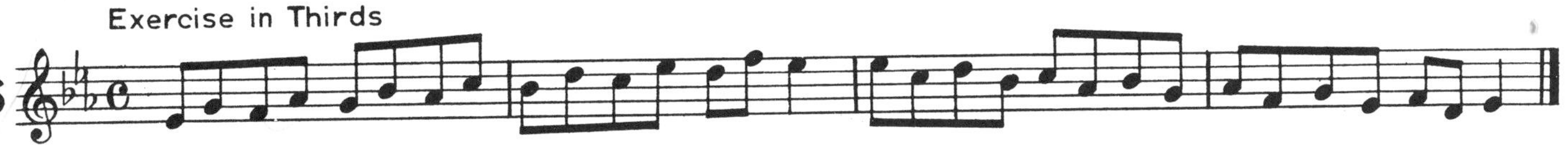

Common Chord

7 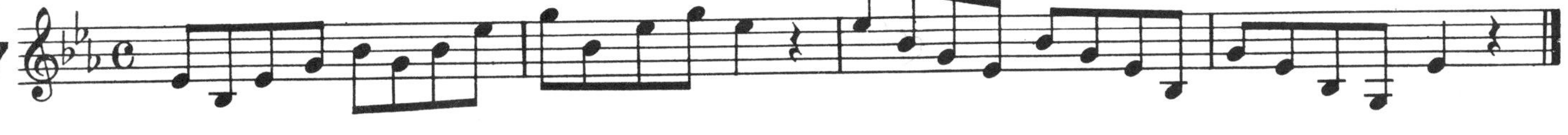

Dominant 7th Chord

8 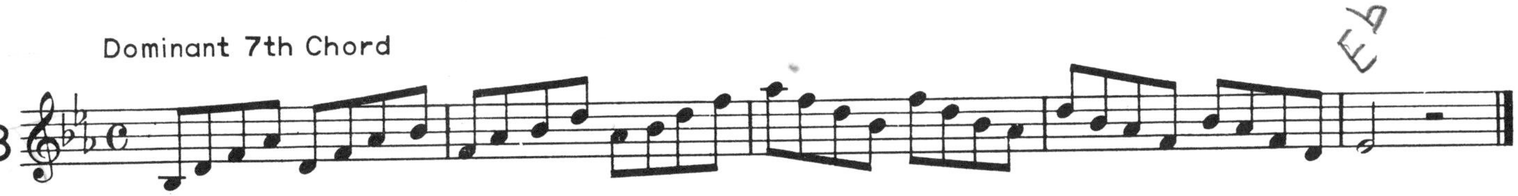

A♭ Major

Studies in Melodic Interpretation
For One or Two Part Playing

The following studies have been selected with the idea of ensemble performance in mind. Much effort has been expended in selecting duets in which the first and second parts are melodically and rhythmically independent. Students should be encouraged to practice these numbers as duets outside of the lesson period. When circumstances permit, any number of students can perform them as an ensemble. The lower part of the duets may be assigned at the discretion of the teacher.

Careful attention to the marks of expression is essential to effective use of the material. Where different dynamic signs are written for the upper and lower parts, observe them accurately. The part having the melody must always slightly predominate even when the dynamic indications are the same.

Pencil the technically difficult passages and devote extra time to their mastery.

In rhythmic music in the more rapid tempi (marches, dances, etc.), tones that are equal divisions of the beat are played somewhat detached (staccato). Tones that equal a beat or are multiples of a beat are held full value. Tones followed by rests are usually held full value. This point should be especially observed in slow music.

Menuet

18th Century

Giga

SPOURNI

3 — Allegro moderato — GATTI

23

GOSTINELLI

4

27
VINCI

Fanfare

NAUDOT

Bourrée

Vivace (♩=80)

18th Century

12

GATTI

Andante cantabile

13

Air
(Lovely Nancy)

Old English

Jigg

Old English

FICINI

GOSTINELLI

19

BOISMORTIER

Vivement (Lively)

21

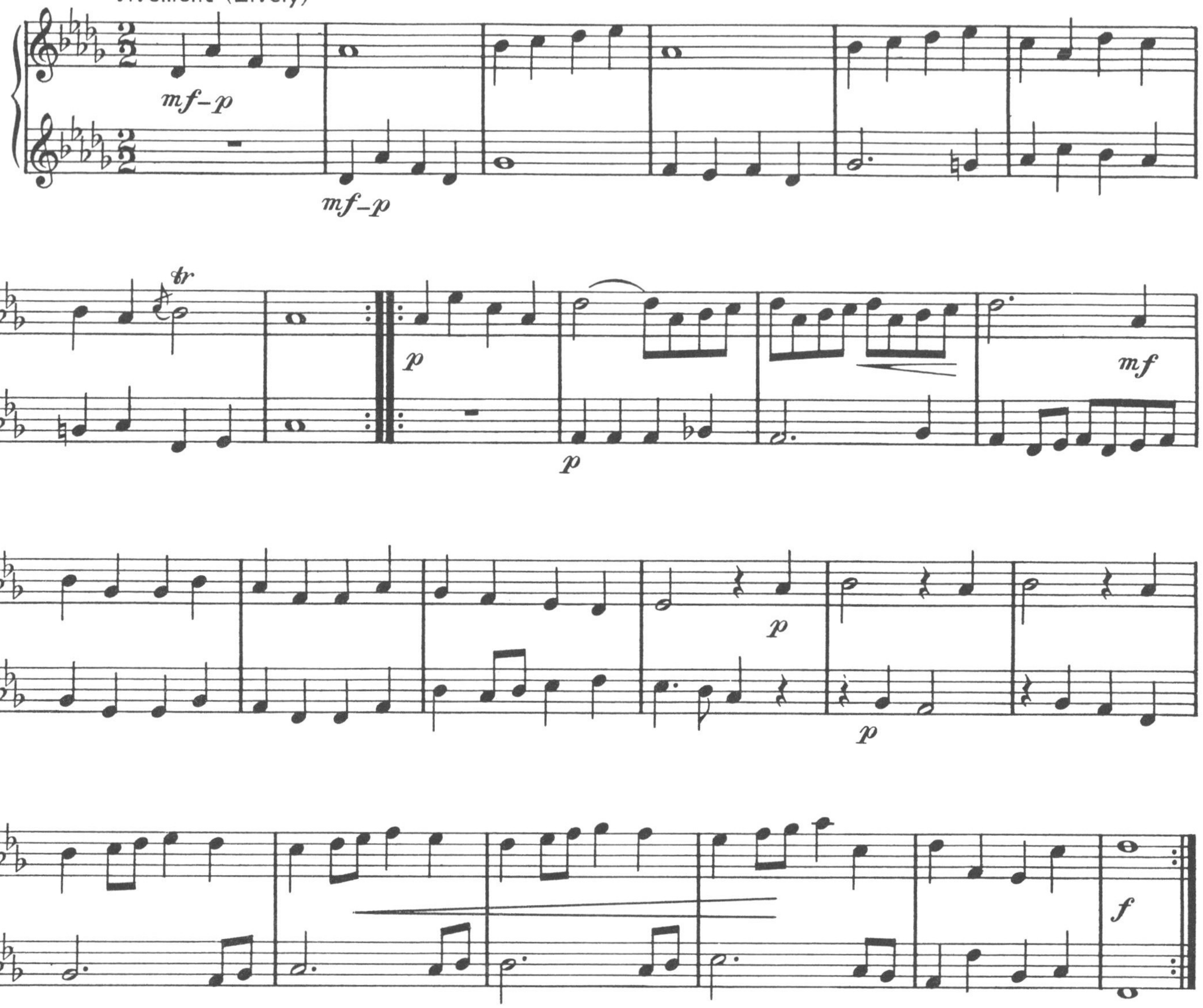

HASSE

Lively

22

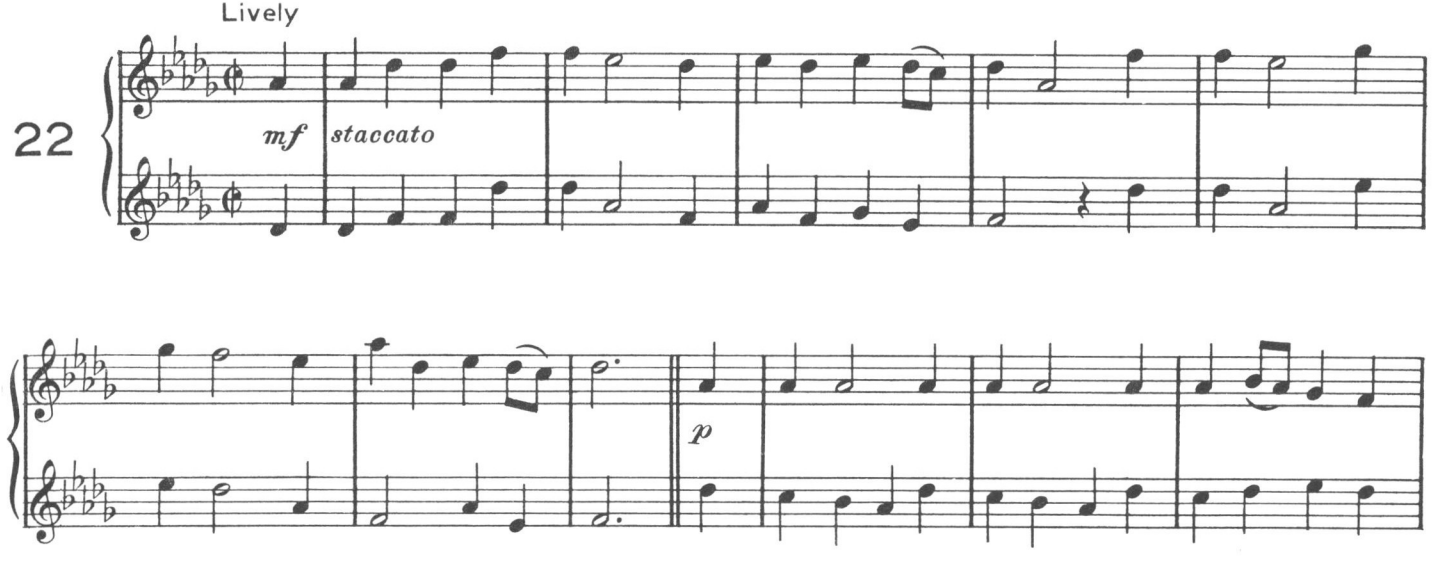

FICINI

HANDEL

Studies in Articulation

The material for this section has been taken for the most part from various standard methods for the Cornet and Trumpet.

Play the exercises as quickly as technic permits unless otherwise indicated.

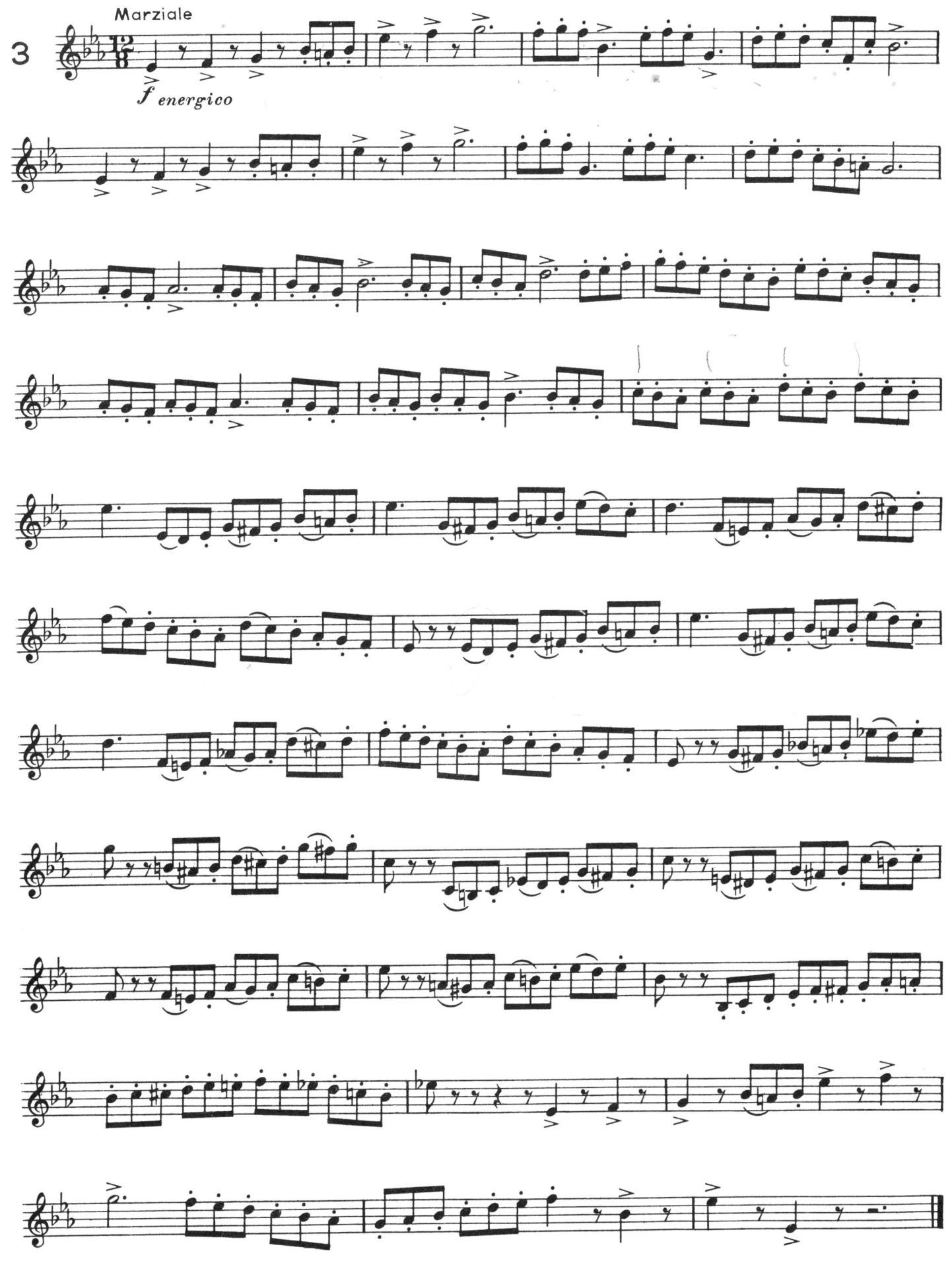

Minuetto

BEETHOVEN

Flexibility Exercises

Tonguing Exercises

TRIPLE TONGUING and DOUBLE TONGUING

Triple tonguing is used when triplets are to be played at a speed that is too fast for single tonguing. The pattern of syllables used for this kind of tonguing is: Tu Tu Ku, Tu Tu Ku, etc.

Double tonguing is used when duplets are to be played at a speed that is too fast for single tonguing. The pattern of syllables in this case is: Tu Ku, Tu Ku, etc.

To develop a technique for either Triple or Double Tonguing it is recommended that the Ku attacks be practiced separately from the Tu attacks until a good tone can be produced on both syllables. The student may then proceed to combine the Tu and Ku, being particularly careful that both syllables sound the same. It is advisable to practice slowly at first in order to produce an evenly articulated rhythm. Increase to a faster tempo only as perfection is reached.

14

DOUBLE TONGUING

(♩= 92 to 160)

15

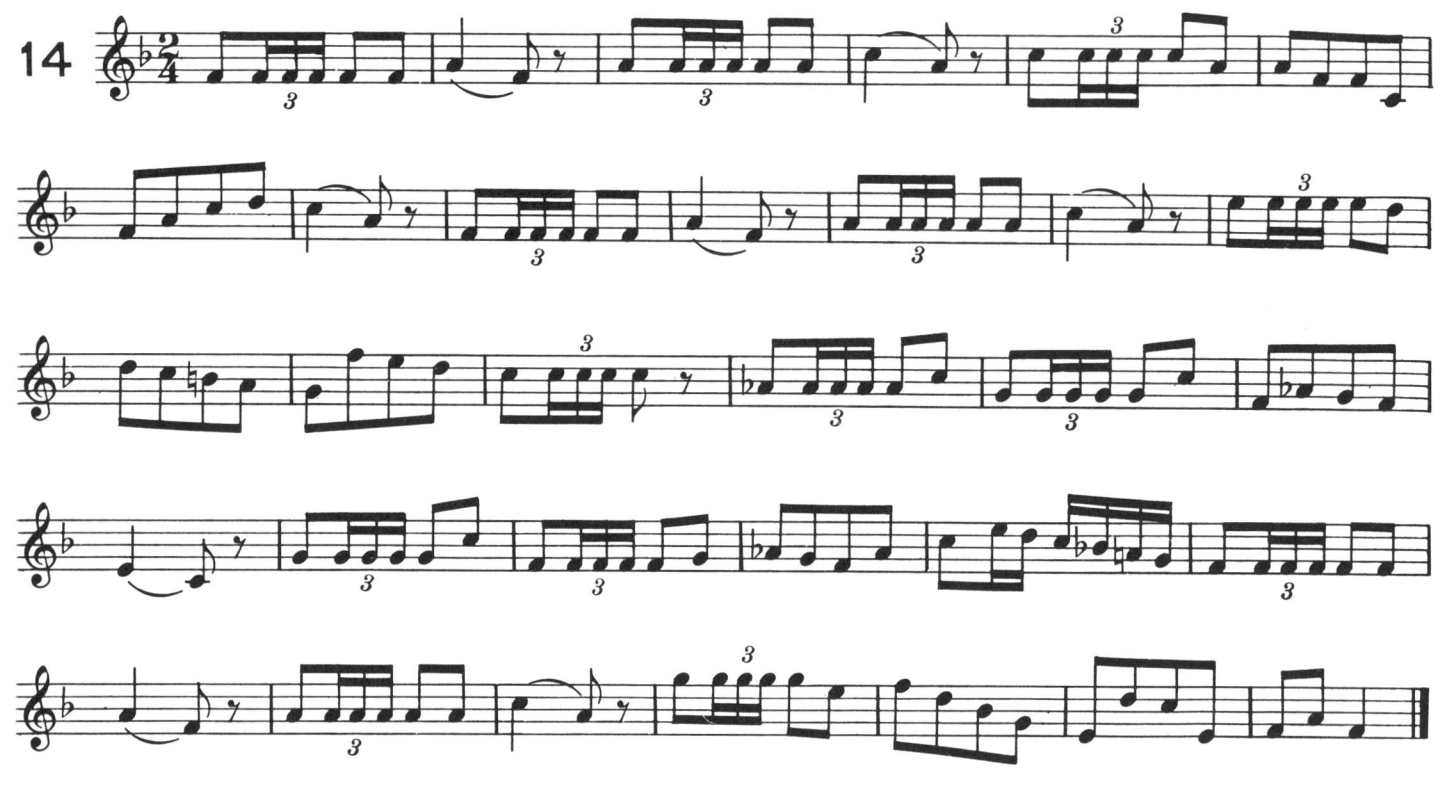

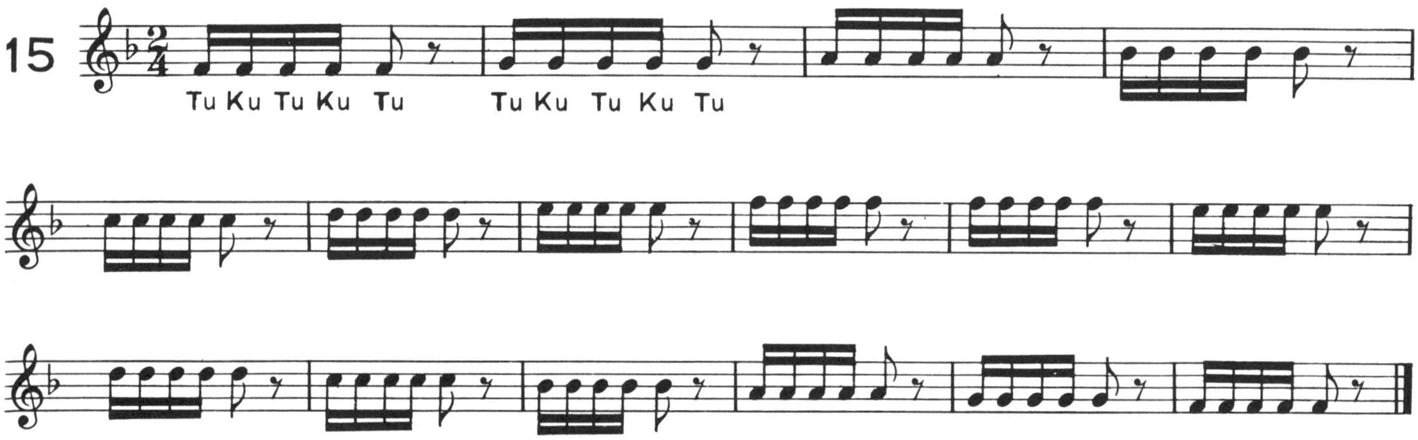

(♩= 96 to 124)

16

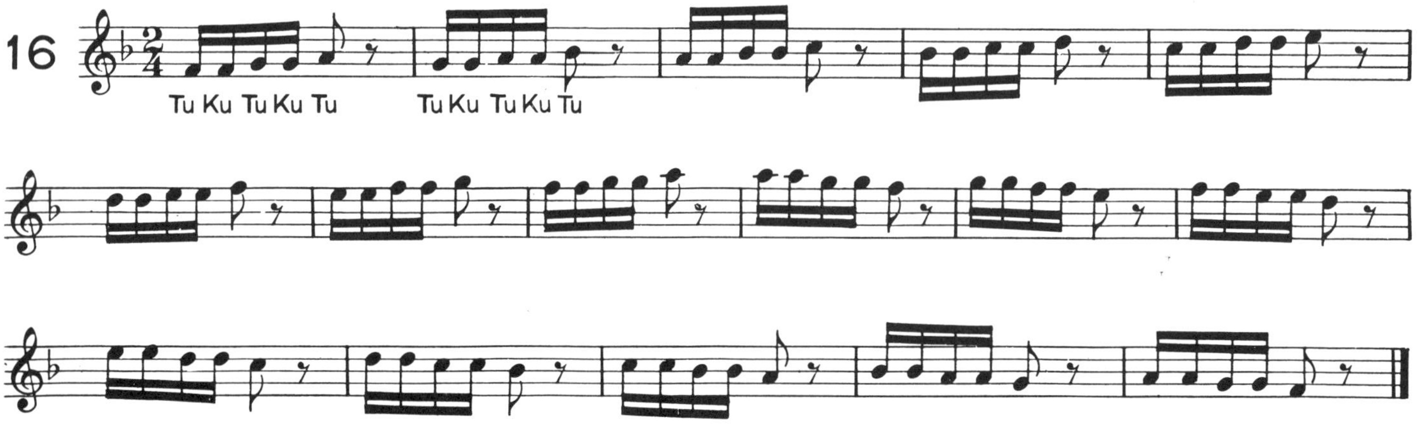

Musical Ornamentation (Embellishments)

ARBAN

Long Grace Notes (Appoggiatura)

The Turn (Gruppetto)

Two Excerpts from "Lohengrin"

In the music of Wagner it is sometimes necessary to play turns that begin on the lower instead of the upper note. The symbol for this inverted turn is ∽. The turn in the excerpt from "Rienzi" was not written thus originally by Wagner but is usually interpreted in the manner indicated.

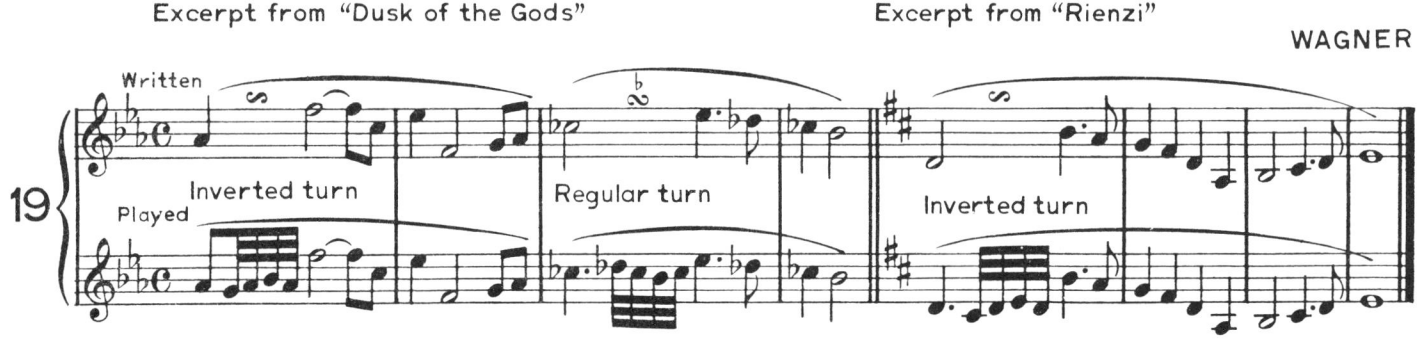

71

Allegro con spirito

ARBAN

20

In the music of the time of Bach and Handel (1685-1759), cadences frequently contain the rhythmic figure  or  . The time value of the dot is not trilled, the execution being  etc. It should be added that the trills of this period should generally begin with the upper note of the trill.

Saraband

CORRETTE

In a stately manner

21

1313-75

SOLOS
Liebeslied

OSKAR BÖHME
Op. 22, No. 2

Morceau de Concours

G. ALARY
Op. 57

NOTE: Piano accompaniments to Nos. 2 and 5 are included in the *Piano book* to the "Concert and Contest Collection for B♭ Cornet or Trumpet."

Andante Cantabile
from "Concerto in E Minor"

MENDELSSOHN
(adapted)

Walther's Prize Song
from "Die Meistersinger"

WAGNER

1313-75

Petite Piéce Concertante

G. BALAY

Valse

SCHUBERT